From Cheese Carrier
to Champion

From Cheese Carrier to Champion

How God Does the Impossible
With the Improbable

F. Austin DeLoach, Jr.

XULON PRESS ELITE

Xulon Press Elite
2301 Lucien Way #415
Maitland, FL 32751
407.339.4217
www.xulonpress.com

Unless otherwise indicated, Scripture quotations taken from the Holy Bible, New Living Translation (NLT). Copyright ©1996, 2004, 2007 by Tyndale House Foundation. Used by permission of Tyndale House Publishers, Inc.

Printed in the United States of America.

ISBN-13: 978-1-5456-6787-3

This book is dedicated to the greatest wife and friend in the world, Jennifer. And also to our daughters, Alora Gail, KenLee, and Dempsey Anna, who have brought a new understanding of love to my vocabulary.

Also, to my father, Austin Sr., and mother, Gail, I thank and love you. Without both of you, this would never have been possible. To my sisters, Stephanie and Ashlee, and their families: You all have blessed my life in so many ways. I am grateful for you.

A special "thank you" to Joey Tucker, Traci Jones, and Janice Daugharty for helping bring this book to completion. I appreciate each of you!

Lastly, to the late Donald and Laurelle Lee. Words cannot express my appreciation for their support.

Table of Contents

Introduction

David and Goliath: these two names are synonymous with hope and overachievement. They are the topic of sermons in the greatest pulpits of our day, and, at the same time, intrigue and excite the hearts of kids in Vacation Bible School and Sunday Schools all around the world.

God has always gotten great glory in taking the improbable and doing the impossible. When Jesus needed to feed five thousand men, not counting women and children, He used a young boy, five barley loaves, and two fish. When God wanted to bring revival and reform to Judah, He used an eight-year-old boy named Josiah. When God wanted a sermon preached that would launch the Church of Jesus Christ into existence, He used an impetuous fisherman named Peter, who had previously denied Him publicly. When God wanted a tough message delivered to the northern tribes of Israel, He called a *sheep breeder and tender of sycamore fruit* named Amos from an obscure village called Tekoa.

In more recent years, God used a man from a farm in North Carolina to reach millions with the gospel. The name *Billy Graham* is known around the world. God also used Jerry Falwell, whose grandfather was an atheist and whose father was an agnostic until near death, to make a difference that is incalculable.

When God needed a big-mouthed, arrogant, but nonetheless undefeated giant defeated, He called a shepherd boy. The event and story of David and Goliath has amazing power because it has a strong emotional appeal, a sense of drama, and deep spiritual meaning. It is a great story because it meets many people of every generation where they live: in need of hope.

Think about it for a moment. The story of one Spirit-filled shepherd boy has, and continues to, touch countless lives. He made a difference because he trusted in God's power and not his own. The fruit of his work on that seemingly hopeless day continues because what he did, he did for the glory of God. Scripture says,

> *Then David said to the Philistine,*
> *'You come to me with a sword, a*
> *spear, and a javelin, but I come*
> *to you in the name of the Lord*
> *of hosts, the God of the armies*
> *of Israel, whom you have taunted.*
> *This day the Lord will deliver*
> *you up into my hands, and I will*
> *strike you down and remove your*
> *head from you. And I will give the*
> *dead bodies of the army of the*
> *Philistines this day to the birds*
> *of the sky and the wild beasts of*
> *the earth, that all the earth may*
> *know that there is a God in Israel,*
> *and that all the assembly may know*
> *that the Lord does not deliver by*
> *sword or by spear; for the battle*
> *is the Lord's and He will give you*
> *into our hands.'*

> — I Samuel 17:45-47 NLT

Even in his early years, David had a passionate love for God and an evident love for life. His struggles were many. Recorded in the same Bible is David's moral collapse with Bathsheba (II Samuel 11) and prideful taking of the census that led to thousands of deaths (II Samuel 24:1-17). This book, though, is written to highlight important principles from one of the greatest stories ever captured: David and Goliath.

I cannot measure the impact David's defeat of Goliath has had on my life. David's courage has served as great motivation for me. There's no question that David's battle with Goliath has encouraged many people who are *facing giants* of their own. Many have attempted and done what seemed to be impossible, inspired by the young shepherd boy.

This book is written to encourage the reader to do exactly as David did: develop a heart for God, be courageous, handle criticism and discouragement, and exceed all expectations for the glory of God.

It is important to understand how this book is written. My attempt is to bring to light important Biblical principles and trust the Spirit of God to practically apply them to your life. My desire is to take the values I see in David's early life and elaborate on them. This book has great potential, not because I wrote it, but because it is rooted in the only book God has written, the Bible.

So, open your heart before you open to the first page. The words you are about to read will hopefully change you. May God bless you during your time of reading and beyond.

Chapter 1

The Rise of David

Our tendency in Bible reading is to only read the *great stories* or *great passages* and allow others to go virtually unnoticed. Take, for instance, John 3:16:

> *For God so loved the world, that He gave His only begotten Son, that whoever believes in Him should not perish, but have eternal life.*

> NASB

This verse is perhaps the most recognizable of all Scriptures, but few people are aware of the wonderful truths that surround it. The two verses that follow state,

> *For God did not send His Son into the world to judge the world, but that the world might be saved through Him. He who believes in Him is not judged; he who does not*

believe has been judged already, because he has not believed in the name of the only begotten Son of God.

— John 3:17-18 NASB

These glorious verses are often hidden in the shadow of John 3:16.

The Biblical account of David and Goliath is one of the most loved and well-known of all Bible stories. However, the story attracts so much attention that few ever read the interesting story that precedes it. Chapter 17 of I Samuel tells the story of David and Goliath in its entirety, but in Chapter 16, the Bible gives great insight as to how David emerged out of obscurity onto the stage of world history.

David is first found in Scripture, alone and a long way, figuratively and literally, from the throne of the Kingdom of Israel. As he is introduced to us in Scripture, he does not seem to be the one the women of Israel would be singing about. But, as the song says, *When others see a shepherd boy, God may see a king.*

Yes, this story seems too good to be true. Saul, Israel's first king, squandered his anointing and was led by one of man's greatest foes, pride. The man who stood head and shoulders in stature above everyone, stooped lower and lower in character. He was a victim, not a beneficiary, of the sowing and reaping principle. He planted pride; he reaped destruction.

Saul's fall moved God's heart to seek another king. Amazingly, God's eye landed on the most unlikely of candidates. It was clear that Saul could not handle the position of king. His blessing became his curse. His outer stature far outweighed his integrity. He ceased serving God and became consumed with personal gain.

There is a lesson to be learned in Saul's fall. Saul took his blessings for granted. He became arrogant. Instead of being a steward of the position God gave him, he desired to be the owner. His approach to the position of king eventually cost him everything, including his life.

So many today find themselves in Saul's condition. Instead of being humbled by the blessings God has given them, their hearts swell with pride. God hates that. His Word promises that destruction will come to the prideful. If God were not so patient, many already would have been destroyed. We should be humbled by God's goodness to us. Tragically, His lovingkindness is often taken for granted. Saul's destruction should serve as our instruction. To be filled with pride invites the chastising hand of God. God's promise is true; the prideful will fall.

Pride goes before destruction, and haughtiness before a fall.

— Proverbs 16:18 NLT

I will not tolerate people who slander their neighbors. I will not endure conceit and pride.

— Psalm 101:5 NLT

All who fear the Lord will hate evil. Therefore, I hate pride and arrogance, corruption and perverse speech.

— Proverbs 8:13 NLT

Pride leads to disgrace, but with humility comes wisdom.

— Proverbs 11:12 NLT

And He gives grace generously. As the Scriptures say, God opposes the proud but gives grace to the humble.

— James 4:6 NLT

The circumstances surrounding David's early life also involved the life of a prominent Old Testament prophet, Samuel. The wise prophet strolled onto the countryside of Bethlehem with a sure word from God. God revealed to Samuel that the king who would take the place of Saul was the son of Jesse in Bethlehem. Samuel did not receive the chosen king's name. He was instructed to go to Jesse's farm and make it known that the next king of Israel was in his household.

It seems that God's reason for not revealing the name of the chosen king was to make a point. The process by which David was revealed is a great story of its own. The lesson of the story: God takes great interest in the condition of the heart. David's humble faithfulness as a shepherd boy paved the road to the palace he would eventually occupy.

When Samuel left on His mission to anoint one of Jesse's sons, he did not go with excitement. The thought of anointing another king while Saul was still alive made no sense to the seasoned prophet. I Samuel 16:1-2 says,

> *Now the Lord said to Samuel, 'You have mourned long enough for Saul, I have rejected him as king of Israel, so fill your flask with olive oil and go to Bethlehem. Find a man named Jesse who lives there, for I have selected one of his sons to be My king.' But Samuel asked, 'How can I do that? If Saul hears about that, he will kill me.'*

> NLT

Obviously, Samuel did not believe God's plan would work. From his standpoint, anointing a new king would not only mark the end of his ministry but also the end of his life. After questioning God's plan, Samuel received this message from the Lord:

> *'Take a heifer with you,' the Lord replied, 'and say that you have come to sacrifice to the Lord. Invite Jesse to the sacrifice, and I*

will show you which of his sons to anoint for me.'

— I Samuel 16:2b-3 NLT

God did for Samuel the same as He does for us. Samuel, as he processed the plan, could not make sense of it. Looking at it from the outside, we can perhaps understand Samuel's reasoning. However, God is never without a plan. And, it is not always reasonable to man.

How many of us have been guilty of questioning the plan God reveals? We say, *Lord, I know you led me to do this, but if I obey You, I just want You to know it is the end for me. I am finished!* We then tell God all the reasons why His plan is not good and why it will not work. After we tell God that He has not thought things through well enough, we should trust the words,

'For I know the plans I have for you...'

— Jeremiah 29:11 NLT

I'm reminded of what God said to Job,

'Who is this that questions my wisdom with such ignorant words?

Brace yourself like a man, because I have some questions for you, and you must answer them. Where were you when I laid the foundations of the earth? Tell Me, if you know so much. Who determined its dimensions and stretched out the surveying line? What supports its foundations, and who laid its cornerstone as the morning stars sang together and all the angels shouted for joy? Who kept the sea inside its boundaries as it burst from the womb, and as I clothed it with clouds and wrapped it in thick darkness?'

— Job 38:2-9 NLT

We know God does not ask questions like this because He doesn't know the answer. These questions reminded Job, and should remind us, that God knows exactly what He is doing.

Many who are called into ministry experience the uncertainty Samuel had. So many who sense the call of God on their lives respond by saying, *God, You have the wrong person. I cannot talk in front of people* (Moses). *I am too young* (Timothy). We offer one excuse after another. When we have offered all the excuses that can possibly be offered and realize that God desires to use us in spite of all the reasons we think He should not, we realize He has a plan, and we are part of it. I like to remind myself, and others, that God knew what He was getting when He called us.

Of course, questioning God's plan is not limited to prophets and preachers. God desires to teach this lesson to all His children. It is not uncommon at all for God to lead a person to do something that does not make sense on the surface. Think about it. It did not make sense to step out of a boat onto a storm-tossed sea, but Peter did (Matthew 14:22-33). It did not make sense for Gideon to narrow his army to 300 men to fight an army with thousands, but he won (Judges 17:17-22). It was laughable to think that Joshua could conquer Jericho by marching around its walls and blowing horns, but the walls fell, and that seemingly unconquerable city was taken (Joshua 6). God's plan often lacks reason. In fact, your own understanding can keep you from the will of God. This must be what inspired the words in Proverbs 3:5,

Trust in the Lord with all your heart; do not depend on your own understanding.

NLT

That's why it is impossible to please God apart from faith. We are not called to walk by sight as followers of Christ. You will never see all God wants you to see walking by sight. God delights in sharing His plan and having His children respond in faithful obedience.

Although Samuel did not fully know how God was going to bring His plan to pass, he obeyed. He arrived in Bethlehem, set up for the sacrifice, and began the search for Jesse's son, the next king of Israel.

The selection process for Israel's second king was intentional. God wanted to make a point. God could have given Samuel the name of the next king. He could have said, *His name is David. Anoint him.* God is not lacking in power to communicate. However, He did not because He was going to use this event as an opportunity to teach a lesson on the importance of having a heart for God. The selection process is most revealing about what is important to God. God did not make this an easy task for Samuel. Faith is not purified in ease but in trial. An untested faith is an untrustworthy faith.

Like Samuel, you may be struggling with an area of obedience in your life. Maybe you cannot understand how God will work it out if you obey what you know He is leading you to do. Perhaps you can't make sense of how you can afford to give what He is leading you to give. Is He calling you into vocational ministry, and you continue to remind Him He has the wrong person? Are you being led out of your comfort zone to an unfamiliar place? The hypotheticals could go on and on. Always remember, obedience to the promptings of God is an option, and it is always the best option we can choose.

Samuel's search began with David's oldest brother, Eliab. Outwardly all indications were he was the most qualified. He was the oldest and, probably, the strongest. He seemed to be the right choice. I Samuel 16:6 tells us how sure Samuel was about Eliab being the logical choice. It states,

Surely this is the Lord's anointed!

NLT

Samuel's conclusion was shallow and fleshly. He based his statement on what he saw with the eyes in his head rather than the eyes of his heart.

This improperly determined conclusion opened the door for God to give the prophet insight on how the second King would be selected. God said to Samuel,

> *'Don't judge by his appearance or height, for I have rejected him. The Lord doesn't see things the way you see them. People judge by outward appearance, but the Lord looks at the heart.'*

> — I Samuel 16:7 NLT

Saul was superior in stature to all in the land (I Samuel 9:2). David, though, had stature that could not be measured with a ruler. His was spiritual. David walked closely with the Lord, but Saul strayed. The Bible says,

> *And the Lord was sorry He had ever made Saul king of Israel.*

> — I Samuel 15:35 NLT

Samuel was getting an unforgettable lesson in trusting God because of Saul's fall and David's rise.

Following the rejection of Eliab, the process of elimination began. Shammah, Abinidab, and the other brothers passed before Samuel, only to be refused by God. The rejection of all the brothers on sight put Samuel in a dilemma. No other brother was physically present, and there had not been any mention that another brother existed. Samuel's trust in God was put to the test once again. He could either ask if another son/brother existed, or he could have given up. Samuel finally asked,

'Are these all the sons you have?'
— I Samuel 16:11 NLT

Put yourself in Samuel's position. While asking Jesse that question was he simultaneously thinking, *What if he says no? Did I really hear from God? Why didn't God just give me the next king's name?* This certainly would have simplified the search process.

Samuel's questioning did not prove to be embarrassing for him, though it might have led to embarrassment for others there.

Jesse's answer allows us to understand the obscurity from which David came. The answer to Samuel's question is no doubt one factor in what makes David one of the most beloved yet unlikely figures in the Bible. Jesse replied,

> *'There is still the youngest. But he's out in the fields watching the sheep and goats.'*
>
> — I Samuel 16:11 NLT

It would have been understandable for Samuel to have thought, *He's keeping sheep. Well, never mind. There's no way the future king is currently in a pasture keeping sheep. Thanks for your time. Bye now!* That's not what happened, though. Scripture records,

> *'Send for him at once,' Samuel said. 'We will not sit down to eat until he arrives.'*
>
> — I Samuel 16:11 NLT

The Bible states that as David stepped into the presence of those gathered, there was no question in Samuel's heart that he was the one. To everyone's astonishment, the Lord said,

'This is the one; anoint him.'

— I Samuel 16:12 NLT

This must have been an emotional moment. It's the kind of moment that brings joy and, I suppose, jealousy. An experience that brings joy to one often sparks jealousy in others. The humility of David was recognized and rewarded. The most unlikely was chosen and anointed. The most improbable thing happened that day, but isn't that just like God?

At this point Samuel's role in the promotion of the new king was ending. I Samuel 16:13 states,

> *So as David stood there among his brothers, Samuel took the flask of olive oil he had brought and anointed David with the oil. And the Spirit of the Lord came powerfully upon David from that day on. Then Samuel returned to Ramah.*

> NLT

Great verse isn't it? The oil of anointing was poured on the new king, shepherd's clothes and all. His brothers watched the unbelievable happen. I'm sure Jesse, David's father, was surprised and overwhelmed with joy. David received God's presence in a powerful way, and the mantle gracefully settled upon him. With the smell of sheep on his hands, he was anointed with oil and the Spirit to become God's chosen man to lead the Kingdom of Israel. God was proven right. Saul did not kill Samuel, as Samuel had feared. The old prophet took his ministry to Ramah with a greater understanding of how important the condition of the heart is to God.

Chapter 16 gives us hope. Do you feel like the least likely to be chosen by God? Remember, while you are faithfully *tending sheep,* God has an eye on you. David shows us the importance of being faithful to God, even if what we are doing seems small. It was David's heart that took him from his flock of sheep to being anointed King, a huge leap indeed. Like David, we can have a heart for God, no matter where we are. Faithfulness to Him today will open doors tomorrow. There will be more on the heart in the final chapter.

Chapter 2

Divine Awareness and Divine Appointments

It's easy to assume David went to the battlefield to fight Goliath. From an earthly standpoint, nothing could be farther from the truth. David did not leave Jesse's farm to fight the champion. He went to the battlefield as a shepherd boy, not a warrior.

Have you ever had a similar experience? You went somewhere for one purpose, only to find that God had another purpose in mind. Take for instance the Day of Pentecost as recorded in the book of Acts. Jews from all over the world gathered in Jerusalem for a celebration, but instead they were there to witness the fulfillment of one of the greatest prophecies in the Bible (Acts 2:17-21). There was also the lame man lying beside the Beautiful Gate. He went there for alms, but he received strength, healing, and salvation (Acts 3:1-10).

This happens with us today as well. In the beauty of God's sovereignty, He can place us exactly where He needs us. We must be aware of this. I like to call it *divine awareness*. Many years ago, when I was a student at Liberty University I experienced this. My roommate and I were watching a football game. He turned to me and said, *Austin, look. That guy just blocked that punt.* So, I watched the replay and, sure enough, the player blocked the punt. Well, I did not really think anything was special about it. I had seen many blocked punts in my life. However, this one would prove to be an instrument God would use to show me His power.

The next day I was to pick up a good friend of mine at the airport in Roanoke, VA. When I got there, I was passing time when a young man approached me. We went through the normal exchange of words. During the course of the initial exchange, he realized I was a Bible student at Liberty. Upon realizing my field of study, he immediately wanted to know if I could help answer questions he had concerning God. I said yes. He (Will) had been raised Catholic. And, for some reason, he had gotten to a place in life where he was searching for answers. He wanted to know the difference between Catholic and Protestant belief. I discussed some of the broader differences, and we made our way to the terminal. As I turned to leave, Will said, *Do you have access to the Roanoke Times? If so, pick up a copy and look on the front page.* I said I did. I could hardly wait to find a copy of that paper. I could not imagine what my new friend possibly wanted me to see.

I bought a copy of the paper, and, to my amazement, there he was, stretched out and blocking a punt. It would not be amazing, except for the fact that he was the player on TV blocking the punt that my friend had pointed out the day before. I thought I was there to pick up a friend at the airport. But that was secondary. God had me there to share with a young man who needed answers. We have schedules, but God makes appointments.

Such was the case with David. He was not on a mission to fight Goliath. Or, was he? It was in the process of a normal mission that David realized his *divine* mission. I Samuel 17:17-18 tells us why David went to the battlefield in the first place:

> *One day Jesse said to David, 'Take this basket of roasted grain and*

these ten loaves of bread, and carry them quickly to your brothers. And give these ten cuts of cheese to their captain. See how your brothers are getting along, and bring back a report on how they are doing.'

NLT

So, there it is. David's earthly task led him to Goliath. Jesse made no mention of fighting. He did not even hint that David was to get involved in the existing conflict between the Israelites and Philistines. The command was simple: take food and bring a report of their condition. It is evident that David's earthly mission was God's way of presenting David his *divine* mission. Jesse's purpose for sending David was God's plan to get His chosen warrior to the battlefield.

When we have the same heart for God that David had, it leads to many opportunities to serve and stand for Christ. We all have daily tasks that need to be fulfilled. Many of these tasks show no evidence of being an opportunity to witness for Christ. God can turn a mundane task into the experience of a lifetime. God is alive and active. He is

THE *Mover and Shaker.* If trained soldiers would not fulfill their responsibility of fighting the mocking giant, God had a young shepherd boy who would.

God proves that He is not impressed with titles and positions. He used a shepherd boy on a lowly task, not the great soldiers of Israel. The titles we can be so proud of are extremely unimpressive to Jesus,

> *who made Himself of no reputation and took upon the form of a servant …*
>
> — Philippians 2:7 KJV

God uses people, not titles; people, not positions. So, wherever you are, or whatever titles you may have (or may not have), you can do great works for God. David was simply an errand-running shepherd boy by title when he first saw Goliath. He did not have the stripes of a decorated soldier. God was not looking for stripes and meaningless titles. He was looking for *a man after His own heart* who would refuse to be intimidated by Goliath.

There may be an opportunity which surfaces for you in the midst of a lowly or routine task. God arranges opportunities for all of us, but to see them, we must have an awareness, a sensitivity to the Spirit of the Lord. It is one thing to be conscious of God in the pew; but when that level of consciousness is carried into the workplace, on airplanes, in meetings, and so on, God opens doors for ministry.

I will never forget a meeting with a realtor concerning a piece of property. I did not know him personally. I was strictly there for business, or so I thought. After we walked through the large building that I was considering for the purpose of housing a future ministry, he made a comment that made me aware that he was a well-known political figure in Georgia. The conversation, much to my pleasure, led from politics to theology. It's almost impossible to discuss one without the other. Can you discuss abortion without factoring in Scripture? As a Christian, is it possible to engage in a meaningful conversation concerning policy to help the poor without consulting Scripture? I digress. My point is that I went there that day to inquire about a piece of land, and I left having witnessed for Christ. We should always be sensitive to what God may want to do in our lives at any given time.

David's arrival at the battlefield was not lacking in action. He had encountered challenges while keeping his father's sheep, but this was war. The Bible states,

> *So David left the sheep with another shepherd and set out early the next morning with gifts, as Jesse had directed him. He arrived at the camp just as the Israelite army was leaving for the battlefield with shouts and battle cries. Soon the Israelite and Philistine forces stood facing each other, army against army. David left his things with the keeper of supplies and hurried out to the ranks to greet his brothers.*
>
> — I Samuel 17:20-22 NLT

Stench of cowardice filled the air. David saw in the Israeli army what Goliath no doubt had already observed: a lack of courage. There were problems on the battlefield. The army of Israel had been paralyzed by one of the most, if not the most, damaging spirits known to man: fear. They were useless pertaining to their mission as soldiers. The taunting voice of the giant had them in a hopeless place. I Samuel 17:23-24 says,

As he was talking with them, Goliath, the Philistine champion of Gath, came out from the Philistine ranks. Then David heard him shout his usual taunt to the army of Israel. As soon as the Israelite army saw him, they began to run away in fright.

NLT

No doubt the sounds of war were a far cry from the serenity of the sheep field for young David. This was war! Lives were at stake. People were shouting. Adrenaline was pumping. And there, in the midst of it all was David, dashing through the mayhem.

David was exactly where God wanted him. This experience was essential to his promotion as king. The earthly mission of his father was instrumental in revealing the mission of his Shepherd in heaven. This is a beautiful picture of the sovereignty of God and the free will of man, together, accomplishing God's divine purpose.

I believe that we are products of the key influences in our lives. This principle has proven true in the shaping of my understanding of God's sovereignty and the free will of man. Since my salvation experience, I have spent a good bit of time around many people who lean heavily toward God's sovereignty or man's free will.

While growing up, my parents would occasionally accompany my grandparents at their church. They were members at a Primitive Baptist church in South Georgia (also known as *foot-washing* Baptist). There are several differences that set the Primitive Baptists apart from others. Primarily, though, the difference is the emphasis the Primitive Baptist Church places on the sovereignty of God in people's salvation and beyond. Most Primitive Baptists, in my opinion, can be considered hyper-Calvinists. Since the original writing of this book, I must admit that it seems many Southern Baptists are leaning that way as well. Hence, the substantial decrease in baptisms. If your theology does not compel you to personally evangelize you should change your theology. I sense many in the modern strand of younger Calvinists are more interested in winning arguments than souls.

My intention here is not to go deep into this discussion. What I have found is that theologians often get so deep they get muddy. That seems to only benefit their pride as people tell them how smart they are. But, few, if any, lives are changed by the prideful exchanges that usually ensue in this debate.

I have witnessed heated arguments among good friends over this subject. I've even engaged in a few. Those who lean too far on either side of this theological fence will at some point fall off. As it relates to this book, let me ask the question, *Who sent David to the battlefield? His earthly father or his Heavenly Father?*

Sadly, Christians can make enemies out of what should be friends. We've seen this happen in the traditional versus contemporary worship war. We see those who lean more towards discipleship often at odds with those who are "more" evangelistic. And, I argue, this is the problem with the free will of man verses the *sovereignty of God* debate. Spurgeon was once asked to reconcile the sovereignty of God and man's free will. He responded, *No, I never reconcile friends.*

So, with that being said, did David go to the battlefield that day because Sovereign God sent him, or did he choose of his free will to go?

The answer: *yes.*

It's impossible to read the Bible without coming away with the understanding that God is sovereign and has all power. However, you cannot read that same Bible without concluding that God has granted to man a free will to obey or disobey Him.

Nothing delights me more than knowing God is sovereign. We can rest in the fact that,

> *God causes everything to work together for the good of those who love God and are called according to His purpose for them.*
>
> — Romans 8:28 NLT

This truth makes it possible for my heart to peacefully sail amidst the turbulent winds of life. It also gives me the hope that at any given moment God can open a major door while fulfilling a minor task. A healthy understanding of God's sovereign power leads to the likelihood of recognizing His divine appointments.

Also, I am most grateful for having a free will. After feeding on the Word of God, prayer and counsel, I have the opportunity to make wise decisions in life. David, on his earthly task and divine mission, made the decision to fight Goliath.

Finally, it is important to understand that God is sovereign; man is not. In His sovereignty He allows us to make decisions, but do not be mistaken. The bottom line is that God can do what He chooses to do. Prayer does change things and authentic faith moves mountains. But, when all is said and done, Praise God! He is the One who is sovereign. We simply have a free will.

David finding his way to Goliath illustrates the way the sovereignty of God and free will of man work together. This was the work of God to get His choice for the next king of Israel in place. God put David into place with the task of carrying cheese to the battlefield. That humble task catapulted David to national recognition and then the palace.

Like David, we must have divine awareness. God often places glorious opportunities in mundane places. I often joke with our church that I pray with more people at the grocery store than I do at the altar. There are no coincidences with Him. He has a plan. A divine plan! And the good news is that

He has chosen to allow us to at least have opportunities in the fulfillment of His purposes. Isn't that great? Your life can make a difference. Never think you just happen to be where you are. God may have a *giant* that needs slaying. He may have you where you are to do it.

The story of David and Goliath is recorded because a young shepherd boy, on a humble errand for his father, was listening to the quiet but loud voice of God among the sounds of war. David was aware of what God was doing. He could have said, *I came here to bring cheese; I did not come to fight*. He did not react that way. Rather, he sensed that God was being mocked. While Jesse, his earthly father, may have given him an earthly mission, God had him on an assignment from heaven.

God has opportunities for you as well. His all-seeing eye and loving-heart can place you in situations of service you never dreamed of. You must be ready to stand when those opportunities arise. Some of the greatest times in your walk with God are when you spontaneously recognize that God has you in a particular place or conversation for an entirely different reason than you had originally thought. That is what happened to David. He *decided* to get involved. David teaches us to be aware of what God may be doing around us. Let God take your mundane tasks and errands and use them to introduce you to His sovereign plan.

One last story: years ago, I pulled up to a gas station on the outskirts of a city in South Georgia. Pumping gas at the tank opposite me was a young lady. I politely spoke to her, and she began to cry. She told me the story of how her kids had been taken from her and the hopelessness she felt. Immediately, I began to try to minister to her and bring some level of peace to her troubled heart. I simply pulled in to get gas. Or did I?

Chapter 3

The Battle Before the Battle

Let no feeling of discouragement prey on you, and in the end you are sure to succeed.

— Abraham Lincoln

I will never forget it. I was attending college in South Georgia. I was immature and unable to deal with the many distractions life can throw your way in your early 20's. So, on somewhat of a whim, I decided I wanted to play baseball again. I had always loved the game, so I walked into the coach's office and told him I would like to try out for the team. I will always remember his response. He said, *Austin, you can try out, but you have a slim to none chance of making the team.*

I also remember one of the most respected teachers in my high school saying to me, *Austin DeLoach, you will never see the day you graduate from college*. Now, in fairness to her, there is no telling what I had done to spark such a comment. I most likely gave many teachers a lot more reason to believe I would be in a chain gang four years after graduation than receiving a college diploma. Still, those words penetrated my heart. I was a sophomore in high school, I think, when that happened. At times, I can still hear her words, even though I graduated from college in 1995.

So often we find ourselves serving as a landing pad for discouraging words. And, at times, we are the launching pad. Receiving discouraging words does not mean we are out of the will of God. Just because someone discourages us certainly does not mean that God does not want us to move forward with whatever we are seeking to do. Rather, discouragement is an inevitable hurdle in life we will have to jump over more than once to get to the desired finish line.

David experienced it. David fought two battles that day. In fact, he may have fought the toughest battle first: the battle of discouragement. Eliab, David's oldest brother, and Saul, the king of Israel, both launched weighty missiles of discouragement towards David.

Upon making his intentions known, David experienced tremendous criticism. He quickly realized what we must all realize: everyone is not for your dream, even if, or, maybe especially if, it is from God. I Samuel 17:28 says,

> *But when David's oldest brother, Eliab, heard David talking to the men he was angry. 'What are you doing here anyway?' He demanded, 'What about those few sheep you're supposed to be taking care of? I know about your pride and deceit. You just want to see the battle.'*

> NLT

Obviously, based on what we already know, this was a false accusation. Not pride, but humility brought David to the battlefield. David was carrying cheese and other food at the request of his father. Also, the phrase *those few sheep* indicates a demeaning spirit from David's eldest brother. In Eliab's eyes, David, the next king, was certainly not capable of keeping more than a *few sheep.* As his oldest brother, Eliab should have already taken up the battle David was about to fight. Was Eliab struggling with being "shown up" by his little brother?

I wonder, though, if it was less of what Eliab said and more of who he was that gave him the potential to affect young David. The slur Eliab made was harsh and, on top of that, not true. David's dangerous trip to the battlefield was to see if Eliab and the other brothers were well. The railing of Goliath revealed Eliab's fear and David's faith.

Eliab, with his potentially devastating false accusation, initiated the first battle David fought. The older brother's critical spirit was perhaps all Satan thought he needed to dampen the fiery faith of David. He was wrong. But, too often, the tactic works.

David withstood the attack of his eldest brother. He remained focused on the task at hand. Eliab's discouragement was unable to distract David. His attempt to derail David only revealed the resolve and resilience of the young shepherd boy. David was able to remain focused on God and His purpose, though Eliab's attack was potent. Withstanding criticism and false accusation is often a necessity if you are going to complete a God-given task.

How can we maintain focus while the missiles of criticism and discouragement are flying all around us? Keep your heart and mind focused on the Lord and what He has called you to do. True purpose gives motivation that is unstoppable by jealous onlookers who have nothing better to do than try to bring others down to their level. John Maxwell says, *Some people criticize so well you would think they are getting paid for it.* Those who live without purpose often desire like-minded company. Living without a purpose, cause, dream, or vision is devastating to the human spirit. People with a sense of purpose will always be under attack from those who do not. *Purposeful people perplex purposeless people.*

As if harsh criticism from his oldest brother was not enough, David had to deal with another round of discouragement before his showdown in the valley with the deranged giant. This time, though, the discouragement would not come in the form of false accusation. Unlike Eliab, Saul's words to David contained truth. The problem with Saul's assessment was that it was void of the power of faith. In essence, Saul said to David: *You can't because you're small. He can because he's large. You can't because you're young. He can because he's older.*

Take a look at Saul's words as recorded in I Samuel 17:31-33:

> *Then David's question was reported to King Saul, and the king sent for him. 'Don't worry about this Philistine,' David told Saul. 'I'll go fight him!' 'Don't be ridiculous!' Saul replied. 'There's no way you can fight this Philistine and possibly win! You're only a boy, and he's been a man of war since his youth.'*

> NLT

As stated earlier, Saul did have his facts right. David was young, small, and inexperienced as a warrior. Goliath was a man of bloody reputation. He had been a warrior for a long time. Reality said David had no chance. Saul's assessment was right, but it had one problem; it did not factor in the fact that,

> *Anything is possible if a person believes.*

> — Mark 9:23b NLT

36

So, David was once again faced with a decision. Was he to believe Saul and forego his intentions or redirect his focus and proceed as planned? He showed the resilience that purpose and faith form when merged in the heart. I Samuel 17:34-37 records David's response:

> But David persisted. 'I have been taking care of my father's sheep and goats,' he said. 'When a lion or a bear comes to steal a lamb from the flock, I go after it with a club and rescue the lamb from its mouth. If the animal turns on me, I catch it by the jaw and club it to death. I have done this to both lions and bears, and I'll do it to this pagan Philistine, too, for he has defied the armies of the living God! The Lord who rescued me from the claws of the lion and the bear will rescue me from this Philistine!'

> NLT

David was ready for the fight. He was not intimidated. His resolve was tested and proven strong. If his oldest brother and the king could not discourage and distract him, no one else could either. The criticism came in two forms. Eliab falsely accused, and Saul was *being realistic*. Neither succeeded.

Eliab attempted to discourage David by using harshness and falsely accusing him. He tried to belittle David. Perhaps he thought if he could successfully discourage David then his younger brother would go back to tending those *few sheep* and stop reminding Eliab of his own cowardice. Personally, I believe bitterness formed in the heart of Eliab when Samuel's oil of anointing was withheld from him and poured on David. David's passionate sense of purpose likely shined light on Eliab's apathy and fear.

It is not my intention to slaughter Eliab in this chapter. However, it is important to understand that Eliab has many clones. Again, Eliab's greatest weapon was not necessarily his words but his position. He was the oldest son, and in the culture of that day, that demanded respect and recognition. Besides that, he was David's big brother. They were family. Eliab was not some unknown soldier. They had the same blood.

I am often amazed at those who feel it is their responsibility to discourage others. I am equally amazed at who, from the standpoint of position, those people are at times. The gravity of criticism is heavy anyway but add to it a close relationship to the source, and the weight intensifies.

Has someone used harshness and false accusation to attempt halting the dream you carry in your heart? Furthermore, has it been someone close to you? Has it been someone you love and even respect? If you have a big dream, one that can only be accomplished by God through you, then it is likely you will face discouragement from people, even some who are close to you.

You may ask, *how do I deal with it?* Going against the grain and believing God to do the impossible seems to attract critics and discouragers. So, what do you do when you find yourself in the crosshairs of critics?

My desire is not to pit you against everyone who criticizes you. There is such a thing as constructive criticism. It often feels like a root canal, but like the root canal, it is very beneficial. That's why it is important to consider the critic, not just the criticism. As stated earlier, I believe

Eliab's criticism came from a bitter heart, sprinkled with jealousy.

David seemed to have easily dealt with Eliab's misguided criticism. David was so focused on the cause that his response to Eliab's slur demonstrates the power of purpose. I have heard it said, *Give me 10 passionate men filled with purpose rather than 100 who only have an interest.* Martin Luther said, *If you have not found something worth dying for then you have yet to live.* That is purpose, and it is the kind the young shepherd boy had.

Many stop mid-stream in the pursuit of dreams because they do not have a true sense of purpose. Living with purpose from God provides the resilience it takes to accomplish great tasks for Him. Quitting is often only the sign of having a minor interest in seeing something happen. Purpose from God is the fuel that moves us to take risks and face uncertainty to see the desired end.

Here is some important advice in dealing with criticism. First, expect it. Then you're not so disappointed when it happens. I like to say, *Budget for criticism at the beginning of the project, because it is coming.* If your dream is large enough and seemingly impossible, expect discouraging words.

Secondly, realize criticism and discouragement can serve as the ultimate test. If the dream in your heart can weather the storm of criticism, it can strengthen you to deal with other challenges that will come your way. Criticism and discouragement often validate or invalidate whether you have received a purpose that originated in the heart of God.

Destructive criticism does not stand a chance when it runs into a person with a true cause. Vague interest will fade at the appearance of criticism, but true purpose will flourish.

David brought more than just cheese and bread to the battlefield that day. He brought passion, purpose, and faith. When he arrived, there were soldiers with swords without faith. David had faith but no sword. We will deal in the next chapter with what it takes to overcome the kind of discouragement David faced with Saul. Let me close this chapter by making this point again. Do not be surprised at discouragement. Rather, be surprised if you do not receive it. Actually, if you do not receive some criticism and discouragement, you may need to check the level of your dream and whether or not it is from God.

Chapter 4

Leveraging the Past

Many people remember what they should forget and forget what they should remember. David retrieved a portion of his past to deal with the discouraging words of Saul. David leveraged his past experiences with God for the good. There is no question, it was God's past work in David's life that largely contributed to the faith he needed to fight off discouragement so that he could fight Goliath.

There is no question that David respected Saul as the king of Israel (I Samuel 24:6). Saul held the highest office in the land. On top of that, he was the first to ever hold that position. It was one thing to be discouraged by his jealous brother in the first round, but the man who held the highest political seat in the land was waiting in the second round.

Again, David was unmoved by the potentially devastating words of the powerful king. David, as is evident in Scripture, held Saul in high esteem. Saul was distinguished, according to Scripture. He would have been the hero of many young, Jewish boys. However, with all his prestige and power, he could not deter the shepherd boy.

David's age and lack of experience in warfare came under attack from Saul. David's response to Saul was different than his response to Eliab, though. As noted earlier, Saul stated facts to David. But David had a set of facts of his own. Right away, Saul pulled out the *age-card* on David:

> *'Don't be ridiculous!' Saul replied. 'There's no way you can fight this Philistine and possibly win! You're only a boy, and he's been a man of war since his youth.'*
>
> — I Samuel 17:33 NLT

How many times has someone been discouraged because of the age factor? Like many, I became a pastor at a young age. I vividly remember being discouraged by an older pastor because of my age.

When I first arrived at the church I have pastored for 22 years, a lifelong member made the comment that she had been in that church longer than I had been alive, and, because of that, I could not tell her anything about the Bible. Without knowing much about me at all, she had drawn a conclusion based on my age. Just a side note, I don't think I was ever able to tell her anything about the Bible.

I assume the *age-old* attack was Paul's reason for writing to Timothy,

> *Do not let anyone think less of you because you are young. Be an example to all believers in what you say, in the way you live, in your love, your faith, and your purity.*
>
> — I Timothy 4:12 NLT

It is presumptuous to criticize a person solely on the basis of age. Scripture gives no indication that God holds a person's age against him/her.

Take, for instance, Josiah. He was eight years old when he became king. Everything was against him. Both his father and grandfather were wicked kings, though his grandfather, Manasseh, did humble himself. But God chose to use Josiah early in life. II Chronicles 34:1 says,

> *Josiah was eight years old when he became king, and he reigned in Jerusalem thirty-one years.*

> NLT

Verse 3a adds,

> *During the eighth year of his reign, while he was still young, Josiah began to seek the God of his ancestor David.*

> NLT

Obviously, Saul took a different approach than Eliab in his attempt to discourage David. As already noted, Eliab's attack was based on big-brotherly surmising. On the other hand, Saul's attack was based on facts.

David's response to Saul's words are powerful and enlightening. To combat the potentially devastating words of Saul, David took a helpful trip down memory lane. He used his past as a source of encouragement:

> *'The Lord who rescued me from the claws of the lion and the bear will rescue me from this Philistine!'*
>
> — I Samuel 17:37a NLT

David's response must have shocked the backslidden king. David spoke of God's faithfulness. He was drawing from his well of experience with the Lord. David saw no reason to conclude that the God who had been faithful to him in the sheep field would be unfaithful to him on the battlefield.

There was an innocence to David sharing such a simple story with the king. I can imagine David's head tilted backward, looking up at the king and, with excitement, recounting his story of God's proven faithfulness.

How often we fail to reflect as David did. We so quickly forget God's past faithfulness. We should build on the times He has proven faithful in the past. We are robbed of so much courage when we carelessly cast our experiences with God into the sea of forgetfulness.

I continuously draw from the well of experiences with God. I will never forget being instantaneously healed as a student at

Liberty University. I left home to head back to college and became so sick with an earache that I pulled over and got a hotel room. God met me in that room. Literally, He healed me in a moment.

After seven years of marriage and days after moving into a brand-new worship center, Jennifer and I separated. Our marriage was hanging by a thread, and it was getting thinner by the day. Only a miracle from God could take the broken pieces left and form a firm foundation. I will never forget God planting a promise from Isaiah 43:18-19 into my heart. At perhaps the most painful part of our separation, I opened God's Word to that verse. It says,

> *Do not call to mind the former things,*
> *Or ponder the things of the past.*
> *Behold, I will do something new,*
> *Now it will spring forth;*
> *Will you not be aware of it?*
> *I will even make a roadway in the wilderness,*
> *Rivers in the desert.*

NASB

There was no question the Holy Spirit led me to that chapter and those verses. God proved Himself faithful again. He changed our hearts and, consequently, changed our home. And He did not waste the trial. What He did in our marriage has opened the door to encourage many marriages. We are beyond grateful.

In September 2016 I received a call from the office of a neurosurgeon. After having an MRI due to minor symptoms, it was determined that I had a tumor the size of a peach near the base of my brain. This led to major brain surgery in September of 2016. I will let the theologian's debate over how the tumor originated. You have some who say God put it there. Others say the devil did it. My surgeon said it had been there since I was in my mother's womb. All I can tell you is who used it. God did! That season of my life changed the way I will experience the seasons I have left.

At one of my first appointments after the surgery, my surgeon said to me, *The grim reaper came for you. It just wasn't your time.* I will never forget God planting Psalms 118:17-18 in my heart. It says,

> *I shall not die, but live,*
> *And tell of the works of*
> *the Lord.*

*The Lord has disciplined me
severely,
But He has not given me over
to death.*

NASB

God used these words to remind me He was going to heal me and give me opportunities to *tell of the works of the Lord*. As always, God was faithful to perform His promise.

Like David's experience with the lion and the bear, these experiences, among others, are in my heart. I can quickly retrieve them. I was reminded, by experience, that God is the ultimate healer of hearts and bodies. I will never forget what God did in that hotel room in South Carolina. It is often that I tell the story about God saving our marriage by changing our hearts. I love to recount the story of all God did in my life in the days leading to brain surgery and the years since. The experiences we have with God should be deposited in our hearts. Then, they can be withdrawn as reminders of God's faithfulness.

I trust you have had experiences with God you can go back to as well. There is an old song that captured my heart many years ago titled, *He'll Do It Again*. The song reviews God's faithfulness in times past: the three Hebrew children in the fiery furnace, Daniel in the lion's den, and Moses. Many of us could add manifestations of God's faithfulness to that song. I know I could.

That's all David was saying to Saul that day. David simply pulled a page out of his *Experiencing God* files and diluted Saul's realistic argument. David gives us great wisdom in his youthful innocence. Having been discouraged by the king with words that were true in content, David placed his spiritual eyes on something that was real to *him*, God's faithfulness. In the wake of Saul telling David the reasons he should not fight the undefeated giant, David revealed to Saul the source of his courage and strength.

There are reasons that keep believers from dealing with discouraging words the way David did. First of all, some conclude God has never performed a miracle in his/her life. Let me assure you, if Jesus Christ and His ultimate act of service on the cross has saved you, you have experienced the greatest miracle of all. I often go back to the moment I repented and turned to Christ. That's the miracle of miracles!

In Mark 2 there is a story that illustrates the miracle of rebirth so well. Four men brought a sick man to Jesus for healing. Instead of first healing him physically, Jesus forgave him of his sins. Jesus went on to heal the man, but He first took care of the man's greatest need: the forgiveness of sins.

The natural tendency of humans is to take God's blessings for granted. David teaches us by example that God's past works in our lives are not to be forgotten but recalled. His past blessings can, and should, serve as reminders of His faithfulness. It is much easier to fight the inevitable foe of discouragement when we stockpile God's past blessings in our weaponry. I am not promoting living in the past, but I am promoting learning from the past and leveraging experiences with God for good.

David had defeated a lion and bear. The Hebrew children experienced the hand of God mightily on their journey: the Red Sea parting, water from a rock, manna from heaven, and the pillar of cloud by day and pillar of fire by night. David gained courage from his miracles, but the Hebrew children had short memories. Exodus 17 records that even after seeing God's hand in such miraculous ways they murmured, complained, and yearned for the days of slavery. In the New Testament (Hebrews 3) God gives a warning for us not to follow in the footsteps of the forgetful Hebrew children.

Think about it. God instated the Passover in the Old Testament because He did not want the Jews to forget what He had done for them. Jesus, our Passover Lamb, began *The Lord's Supper* because He never wants us to forget His shed blood and broken body. Look closely at I Corinthians 11:23-25. Notice the word *remembrance*:

> *For I received from the Lord that which I also delivered to you, that the Lord Jesus in the night in which he was betrayed took bread; and when He had given thanks, He broke it, and said, 'This is My body, which is for you; do this in remembrance of Me.' In the same way He took the cup also, after supper, saying, 'This cup is the new covenant in My blood; do this, as often as you drink it, in remembrance of Me.'*

> NASB

If you have taken the wonderful blessings of God for granted and failed to draw strength and courage from what He has done for you, I have good news for you. You can turn past victories into faith blocks and build a fortified wall that will stand against the discouraging words you will face in life. Stop taking all He has done for you for granted. Do not allow your dreams to crumble under the words of your discouragers.

Chapter 5

Revisiting the Past

Most of us have felt the shame and guilt of past sins and failures. For some, it remains like a dark cloud. I know that memories of some of my past actions have, at times, been very hard to deal with.

When we dwell on the sins and failures of our past, it is impossible to walk in the freedom Christ made possible by His more than sufficient payment on the cross. I want to take this chapter and continue to discuss the past because, unlike David, who used the past to encourage himself, many of us have allowed our past to become less our friend and more our enemy. Putting the past in its place is essential for those who desire to live the abundant life Jesus said He came to give.

When writing about the past, I cannot help but think of Doug Heard. I had the blessing of leading Doug to Christ in the mid-1990's.

Doug had paved a wide road of sin early
in his life. He was known for bar room
brawls. While all sin separates us from
God, it cannot be denied that some create
more baggage than others. Doug definitely
had his share.

Doug got it. You may say, *Got what?* The
gospel! He got the Good News. He never got
over being under God's spout of grace. It
was nothing for this man's man to tear up
when the name *Jesus* was mentioned. Many
lives were changed as a result of his
changed life. Doug's sin was great. Jesus'
grace was greater.

Your past can be used for good. You may
be saying, *But you don't know what I've
done.* You are right, but I know what Christ
has done. He has paid the sin debt of the
world in full. Had God intended for you to
live under the guilt and condemnation of
past sins, He never would have gone to the
length He did for you to be forgiven. God
does not want you to live with a spirit of
condemnation. Rather, he desires for you
to live in the freedom that true forgiveness brings.

Jesus makes it clear in John 3:17-18 that, because of Him, no one has to be loaded with guilt and condemnation. He said,

> *For God did not send the Son into the world to judge the world, but that the world might be saved through Him. He who believes in Him is not judged; he who does not believe has been judged already, because he has not believed in the name of the only begotten Son of God.*
>
> NASB

When you trust Christ with saving faith, there is no reason to live under a cloud of condemnation. We will be chastised but not condemned. Jesus did not come to intensify shame; He came to eliminate it.

For so many, the past is like a ball and chain that is keeping them from advancing toward what God wants to do in their lives. As a pastor, it breaks my heart to preach the beauty of the gospel and see people continue drowning in a sea of guilt.

Here's the point: I cannot change the actions of my past, and neither can you. Whatever you do, please settle this issue.

What has been done has been done. Life is progressive not regressive. Your future will one day be your past, not vice-versa.

Let me take you back to the original intent of this chapter: in his bout with Goliath, David leveraged his past in a way that contributed to his victory. How about you? Is your past hindering or helping you?

I have regrets in life. I have never been one that enjoys talking about my past sins and failures. Sometimes, oddly enough, you hear supposed Christians proudly comparing their sinful pasts. To me, there is something wrong with that picture. There is nothing particularly gratifying to me about actions that contributed to hanging Jesus Christ on the cross.

Regret, however, should not be confused with guilt. There are actions that, given the opportunity, I would not do if given another chance. But I refuse to spend one moment sulking in guilt over repented sins. Romans 8:1 says,

> *So now there is no condemnation for those who belong to Jesus Christ.*

NLT

Condemnation and guilt are paralyzing to the spirit. Living in bondage to your failures will hinder your effectiveness for God and the joy He desires for His people. Paul understood very well the importance of his past.

In Philippians 3:13-14, Paul clearly helps us understand his view of his past. He wrote,

> *No, dear brothers and sisters, I have not achieved it, but I focus on one thing: Forgetting the past and looking forward to what lies ahead, I press on to reach the end of the race and receive the heavenly prize for which God, through Christ Jesus, is calling us.*
>
> NLT

At the time of the original writing of this book, Josh, my wife's brother, and I watched a portion of the Olympic games. Michael Johnson ran like the wind to win the 400-meter race. His strides were smooth and measured. That race makes for a perfect illustration of this point. Suppose Johnson would have said just before the race began, *Get a ball and chain and tie it to my waist. I am going to drag it to the finish line.*

As silly as that may sound, many people who read this book are dragging their past around like a ball and chain and will fail to run the race of life the way God would have it to be run. This is what the writer of Hebrews had in mind when writing,

> *Therefore, since we are surrounded by such a huge crowd of witnesses to the life of faith, let us strip off every weight that slows us down, especially the sin that so easily trips us up. And let us run with endurance the race God has set before us.*

— Hebrews 12:1 NLT

The Apostle Paul, whose past included supporting the slaying of Christians and persecution of the early church, said his plan was to forget the past and focus on the future. His reputation went before him. Ananias feared Paul because of his reputation. His words are recorded in Acts 9:13:

> *'But Lord,' exclaimed Ananias, 'I've heard many people talk about the terrible things this man has done to the believers in Jerusalem.'*

NLT

Still, Paul did not allow the depth of his notorious sins to drown him in guilt.

There is only one way to put guilt and condemnation to rest. No matter how extensive your past failures and sins may have been, you do not have to be spiritually handcuffed to them for the rest of your life. Certainly, there are consequences to sin that may last for a while, if not a lifetime. However, dealing with the consequences of sin and living under its dominion is different; or at least it should be. God's grace is available to us to enable us to deal with the ramifications of past sins as well; another reason we call it *Amazing Grace*.

The greatest example of this is David and his adulterous affair with Bathsheba, which resulted in her pregnancy. This is a tough truth, but the child died as a result of the sin of David and Bathsheba. Recorded in II Samuel 12:13-14 are Nathan's words to David:

> *Nathan replied, 'Yes, but the Lord has forgiven you, and you won't die for this sin. Nevertheless, because you have shown utter*

contempt for the word of the Lord by doing this, your child will die.'

NLT

We must guard against using this story in a way that makes people believe that every traumatic experience is the result of a specific sin. Jesus dealt with this faulty concept in the New Testament when He was asked if a child who had been born blind was the result of a specific sin. John 9:1-3 says,

> *As Jesus was walking along, He saw a man who had been blind from birth. 'Rabbi,' His disciples asked Him, 'why was this man born blind? Was it because of his own sins or his parents' sins?' 'It was not because of his sins or his parents' sins,' Jesus answered. 'This happened so the power of God could be seen in him.'*

NLT

The loss of David's child was the result of his sin with Bathsheba. According to the Scripture, the child died specifically because of David's actions. With great blessings come great responsibility and accountability.

After getting word from the prophet that his child would die, David prayed and fasted for God to allow the child to live. Upon hearing the news of the child's death, the Bible says,

> When David saw them whispering, he realized what had happened. 'Is the child dead?' He asked. 'Yes,' they replied, 'he is dead.' Then David got up from the ground, washed himself, put on lotions, and changed his clothes. He went to the Tabernacle and worshipped the Lord. After that, he returned to the palace and was served food and ate. His advisors were amazed. 'We don't understand you,' they told him. 'While the child was still living, you wept and refused to eat. But now that the child is dead, you have stopped your mourning and are eating again.' David replied, 'I fasted and wept while the child was alive, for I said, Perhaps the Lord will be gracious to me and let the child

live. But why should I fast when he is dead? Can I bring him back again? I will go to him one day, but he cannot return to me.'

— II Samuel 12:19-23 NLT

This exchange illustrates the previous point well. David sinned and brought pain to many. After being so blessed by God, David caved into the mounting pressure of temptation and suffered the consequences.

The passage of Scripture just read might cause you to think of David as being heartless. He prayed for the child to live, but that did not happen. The Bible says that immediately after the child's death, David got up, anointed himself, changed clothes, and headed to the house of the Lord. One may say, *What a reaction to the death of a child!*

But do not be so quick to pull the trigger on David. I would never make light of the death of a child, but it is important to understand the way David repented of his sin and pressed forward.

I can hear the critics saying, *You are making light of sin. You must be one of* those *'cotton candy' preachers*. Let me say again for the sake of emphasis: what David did with Bathsheba and the subsequent cover-up was sin. He lost the joy of his salvation and his integrity to effectively witness for God. He was guilty of murder, adultery, severe injustice, and abuse of power. The consequences of his sin remained for years.

Still, take human emotion away for a moment and look at what happened. David repented. He sought God for forgiveness and restoration. And then he focused on the future. His servants said,

> *'You have stopped your mourning and are eating again.'*

> — II Samuel 12:21 NLT

I believe David's response indicated he had done all he could to save the life of the child. He accepted the consequences. He looked ahead to seeing him again. But he got up, got dressed, and moved forward.

There is no reason to believe David did not regret what he had done. Psalm 51, his prayer of repentance, certainly indicates there was heartfelt conviction for his sin.

Again, David got up, cleaned up, looked up, and moved forward by the mercy of God (Psalms 51:1).

People try to deal with guilt in many ways. Some turn to drugs, alcohol, excessive work, or multiple relationships just to cope. Actually, so many of the ways people attempt to deal with guilt from the past only contribute more guilt. The only remedy for living under the cloud of guilt and shame is a proper understanding of the grace of God.

So, right here, you may want to stop reading for a moment. Perhaps you are tired of your past weighing you down. Why don't you say once and for all,

> *God, I have sinned. I have asked you many times for forgiveness but have never stopped living under the dominion of guilt. Right now, I want to thank You for forgiving me, for not condemning me. Because of what you have done for me, I am going to cease living in the grip of condemnation. Thank you for freedom. I am ready to press forward toward the mark for You. In Jesus' name, Amen.*

Now that you have determined to move on, your life will be much different. Your past can now serve as a testimony of grace rather than a millstone of guilt. Please remember God's forgiveness is complete. God loves a truly repentant heart. A broken heart receives the healing balm of forgiveness. Let's go back once more to the original purpose of this chapter. David's past served him well in fulfilling his purpose. He was motivated in the present by what God had done for him in the past. Now, you can be as well. It's time to move forward. It is time, as William Cowper penned, to enjoy the pleasure of knowing the stain of your sin is no match for the detergent of Christ's blood:

> *There is a fountain filled with blood*
> *Drawn from Immanuel's veins;*
> *And sinners, plunged beneath that*
> *flood, Lose all their guilty stains:*

Chapter 6

Faith:
The Mover of God's Heart

One of the highlights of my ministry was a few days I was able to spend with Dr. Elmer Towns. Dr. Towns is the co-founder of Liberty University and has authored over 100 books. Eight of his books are on the *Best-sellers List for the Christian Booksellers Association*. He came to our church for a seminar. I had a lot of questions, and he had a lot of answers.

In the New Testament the question was asked of Jesus,

> *'Teacher, which is the most important commandment in the law of Moses?'*

> — Matthew 22:36 NLT

Like those who asked this question, I had a question for Dr. Towns that was similar in its approach. I wanted a simple answer to a rather broad question. I asked Dr. Towns, *What is the common thread that runs through everyone that God has greatly used?*

I could not wait to hear his answer. Would it be *integrity*? Would it be *knowledge*? Would it be *charisma*? I wondered if there was one characteristic he had noticed that was essential. I will never forget his answer, or the confidence with which he said it. He replied, *Faith!* It was as simple as that. He then gave me a list of modern examples of people who have trusted God and seen great results. Looking back, I can see how true Dr. Towns' answer was. This truth also presents itself in the story of David and Goliath.

Not many, if any, would have blamed David had he taken the advice of King Saul. Saul was the one who tried to persuade David not to fight the giant because he felt the young shepherd boy was, to say the least, ill-equipped to deal with such a formidable foe.

Interestingly, after trying to discourage David from fighting Goliath, Saul then tried to give him armor for the battle. The Bible says in I Samuel 17:38-40:

> *Then Saul gave David his own armor — a bronze helmet and a coat of mail. David put it on, strapped the sword over it, and took a step or two to see what it was like, for he had never worn such things before. 'I can't go in these,' he protested to Saul. 'I'm not used to them.' So, David took them off again. He picked up five smooth stones from a stream and put them in his shepherd's bag. Then, armed only with his shepherd's staff and sling, he started across the valley to fight the Philistine.*

> NLT

This was certainly an interesting turn of events. The king attempted to suit the young shepherd boy with his armor. David refused it. It did not fit. But David had armor that could not be seen. We will soon learn that David had a shield; it was named *faith*. David had a sword; it was the Word of God.

The true giants we face in life are only defeated by faith in God. When I say faith,

Furthermore, this is not a self-help story. David yielded *self* to God. He did not do this on his own. Remember, Paul did not say, *I can do all things.* That's secular. That's what the world says. No. Paul said,

> *For I can do everything through Christ, who gives me strength.*
>
> — Philippians 4:13 NLT

The Bible does not say, *nothing will be impossible.* It says,

> *For nothing will be impossible with God.*
>
> — Luke 1:37 NASB

Without God, David did not stand a chance to defeat Goliath. But, with God, Goliath did not stand a chance. Faith is the difference maker. David made it clear. God would bring the victory. It was faith that allowed David to be an instrument through whom God would work.

David was not trying to draw attention to himself with idle talk. He was NOT *all talk and no action.* He possessed the kind of faith that inevitably results in works. David gathered five smooth stones. Had he lost his mind? Without the benefit of a soldier's armor, he knelt down, opened up his shepherd's bag, and dropped in his ammunition.

> *He picked up five smooth stones from a stream and put them into his shepherd's bag. Then, armed only with his shepherd's staff and sling, he started across the valley to fight the Philistine.*
>
> — I Samuel 17:40 NLT

Can you imagine this scene? David did not look like a warrior; rather, he was most likely decked out in shepherd's clothing: a staff, a shepherd's bag, and a sling. Was he just an overzealous lad who stumbled upon a situation that had his emotions aroused to the point he was out of touch with common sense? The answer is no. The faith David possessed in God caused him to NOT limit his life to what seemed logical. Once again, Solomon reminds us in Proverbs 3:5,

> *Trust in the Lord with all your heart; do not depend on your own understanding.*
>
> NLT

Those who walk by faith do not idly watch as opportunities pass by. Faith in God brings courage that propels people past doing what is easy and moves them to do what is necessary to fulfill God's plan here on earth. Stepping out into rough waters is not uncommon for those who choose to walk by faith.

Loving and trusting God compelled David to do what apathy and fear could not motivate the soldiers to do. Faith works. Faith moves the heart of God. Then He moves His hand. Faith allows us to see what others cannot see, and, consequently, accomplish what others cannot accomplish.

The story of David and Goliath would be a huge let down had David talked about what he was going to do only to back out at the end. Proverbs 14:23 states,

> *Work brings profit, But mere talk leads to poverty!*
>
> NLT

David was not there to *merely talk*. He picked up stones, prepared himself, and approached Goliath.

Often, we see the opposite take place. We state our intentions. On an emotional whim, we talk of dreams and visions that never come to pass. Many have talked about writing a book. Many have had plans for years to launch a ministry or business. Many have talked about going back to school to finish that degree. As a pastor, I have heard many people talk about what they were going to do. John Maxwell says, *When all is said and done, there is usually more said than done.* When David armed himself and began to run toward the bloodthirsty giant, it was proof that he had not been idly talking. The proof of his faith was in what he did, not what he said. This is a great place to consider what James said about faith and works:

> *So, you see, faith by itself isn't enough. Unless it produces good deeds, it is dead and useless. Now, someone may argue, 'Some people have faith; others have deeds.' But I say, 'How can you show me your faith if you don't have good deeds? I will show you my faith by my good deeds.'*
>
> *— James 2:17-18 NLT*

Do you have a living or dead faith? That question can only be answered by determining if the faith you have is leading you to walk out onto some battlefields in life, where the giants are. Do you ever bypass your own understanding to answer the call of God? I praise God that works do not save us, but we should be workers because of our faith. Many people only read Ephesians 2:8-9. But, take a look at the entirety of what Paul said concerning grace and works:

> *For by grace you have been saved through faith; and that not of yourselves, it is the gift of God; not as a result of works, so that no one may boast. For we are His workmanship, created in Christ Jesus for good works, which God prepared beforehand so that we would walk in them.*
>
> *— Ephesians 2:8-10 NASB*

James simplifies this principle by stating,

> *If a brother or sister is without clothing and in need of daily food, and one of you says to them, 'Go in peace, be warmed and be filled,' and yet you do not give them what*

*is necessary for their body, what
use is that?*

— James 2:15-16 NASB

Talk alone is not the stuff faith is made of.
Have you been talking more than doing? In
dealing with this topic, care must be taken
to not give people a works-based understanding of salvation. Saving faith will
call us to action. Biblical faith leaves
no room for apathy. David was a dreamer.
He was also a doer. We need dreamers who
wake up and do the works God has prepared
for them and prepared them for.

Dead faith only allows a person to experience in life those accomplishments that
can be gained by human strength. If you
don't need God to accomplish your dream,
it most likely did not originate in heaven.
God desires for us to possess the kind of
faith that will launch us out into the deep
so that we no longer place our faith in
the shoreline but in Him (Luke 5:4-5). We
need faith that will give us the courage
to walk into the fiery furnaces of life
without fearing the consequences (Daniel
3:17-18). We need faith that will take
mountains and cast them into the depths
of the sea (Matthew 21:21). True faith

affords us opportunities to see God work in ways that only He can get the glory for. It lets us see the intimidating giants of life fall.

There was an intangible on the battlefield that day. A mistake that Goliath made was viewing David simply from a physical stand-point. I Samuel 17:41-42 states,

> *Goliath walked toward David with his shield bearer ahead of him, sneering in contempt at this rud-dy-faced boy. 'Am I a dog,' he roared at David, 'that you come to me with a stick?' And he cursed David by the name of his gods.*

NLT

Goliath made the same mistake others had made about David. He underestimated him. He was used to shouting his taunts and sol-diers running. But David did not run away from him. He ran to him.

Goliath was insulted. David did not seem to present any kind of challenge for the undefeated champion. Faith itself cannot be seen, but Biblical faith always has vis-ible effects. Goliath fell because of faith.

He thought he was fighting David. Actually, he was fighting the faith of David and, consequently, the God of David. Goliath did not know it, but he was the true underdog.

Intimidation is one of Satan's powerful tools. The Bible says,

> *Stay alert! Watch out for your great enemy, the devil. He prowls around like a roaring lion, looking for someone to devour.*

> — I Peter 5:8 NLT

He roars. He attempts to frighten. He paralyzes with fear. There is a reason the Bible repeatedly warns against being afraid. Paul even reminded Timothy,

> *For God has not given us a spirit of fear and timidity, but of power, love, and self-discipline.*

> — II Timothy 1:7 NLT

Understand this — Goliath lied. Nothing he said came to pass. He did not feed David to the birds or beasts. His taunting words revealed fear in the soldiers. Those same words highlighted the faith of the shepherd boy.

This tactic is demonstrative of Satan himself. His weaponry is full of deceit. In John 8:44 Jesus stated,

> *'For you are the children of your father the devil, and you love to do the evil things he does. He was a murderer from the beginning. He has always hated the truth, because there is no truth in him. When he lies, it is consistent with his character; for he is a liar and the father of lies.'*

> NLT

Has Satan shot his darts of deceit your way? Have you been paralyzed by worry and fear? It happens, and it happens often. He no more wants you to defeat the giants in your path than he wanted David to defeat Goliath.

Goliath's words landed on the heart of young David. This time Goliath faced courage, not cowardice. No longer could he play the part of the bully on the schoolyard playground. David had humble confidence not haughty arrogance.

The confidence David possessed must not be mistaken for pride and arrogance. Pride precedes destruction (Proverbs 16:18). Nowhere is that truth better proven than in the story of David and Goliath. David's confidence was an overflow of his faith in God. Goliath was the poster child of self-confidence. David was not self-confident. He was God confident. Pride (Goliath) met humility (David). Pride was destroyed (Proverbs 16:18) and humility was exalted (I Peter 5:6). Look at David's confident response to Goliath's weightless threats:

David replied to the Philistine, 'You come to me with sword, spear, and javelin, but I come to you in the name of the Lord of Heaven's Armies — the God of the Armies of Israel, whom you have defied. Today the Lord will conquer you, and I will kill you and cut off your head. And then I will give the dead bodies of your men to the birds and wild animals, and the whole world will know that there is a God in Israel! And everyone assembled here will know that the Lord rescues His people, but not with sword and spear. This is the

*Lord's battle, and He will give
you to us!'*

— I Samuel 17:45-47 NLT

Did you read closely what David said? The
victory would cause others to know that
there is a God in Israel. David did not
say the victory would show that there was
a great, confident warrior in Israel. Even
before the fight, David gave the glory to
God. David said,

> *'I come to you in the name of the
> Lord of Heaven's Armies — the God
> of the armies of Israel, whom you
> have defied.'*

— I Samuel 17:45 NLT

What if David had said, *I come to you in
the name of David.* David wanted all to know
that, although it appeared to be, it was not
a battle between *David and Goliath.* This
battle was between God and Goliath. David,
by faith, gave the battle to the Lord. That
is a whole new perspective, isn't it?

Of course, David was there. He appeared to
be the one in the fight. And, in a sense,

he was. Empowering the young shepherd boy, though, was God.

Not many onlookers, if any, believed David would win the battle. Maybe there were a few who liked to go against the odds, but all outward indicators gave the victory to Goliath. Suffice it to say, Vegas would have given David no shot.

There is an important lesson here about facing our own giants. No matter what kind of power your giant may pack, it is no match for the God who dwells within you. Goliath's sword and spear were no contest for David. Isaiah 54:17 reminds us,

> 'No weapon that is formed against you will prosper; And every tongue that accuses you in judgement you will condemn. This is the heritage of the servants of the Lord, And their vindication is from Me,' declares the Lord.

> NASB

The weapons of this world are powerless before God. David knew that. Goliath's impressive arsenal did not dampen David's fiery faith. God was for David. And, Paul reminds us,

> What shall we say about such wonderful things as these? If God is for us, who can ever be against us.
>
> — Romans 8:31 NLT

That verse has often been paraphrased, *If God be for us, everyone else might as well be.* Numbers, power, and reputation melt in the presence of Almighty God. It is true,

> The horse is prepared for the day of battle, but the victory belongs to the Lord.
>
> — Proverbs 21:31 NLT

Like David, make all the preparations you can. He picked up the stones. He fought off discouragement. He loaded his sling. He ran to the battlefield. All of that is true, but, make no mistake about it, the Lord gave him the victory!

Chapter 7

Influence: Moving Others to Action

Before leaving for Bible college, I worked for an organization in my hometown that helped serve the needs of handicapped people. I loved my job. There were tough days, but people, in spite of, and because of their physical condition, taught me about true love.

There was one in particular. His name was Junior, and he had Down's Syndrome. He is no longer here on earth, but his influence will live at least as long as I do. Junior influenced me with his kind, compassionate heart. His smile was so encouraging. I can still see it to this day in my mind's eye.

Junior had not read leadership books on how to influence people. Nevertheless, my memories of him caused me to want to live a life filled with love and kindness. He could not communicate words of great wisdom, but when he smiled so big, his eyes squeezed shut, and he communicated something that was beyond the capacity of words. Again, I can see him approaching me with his arms wide open. He was a mover and a shaker. I cannot get over the effect he had on my life. Maybe today he is peering over the balcony of heaven and smiling that smile with the full knowledge of the impact God allowed him to have. That is the nature of influence. Our lives have the potential at times to touch people, and we are not even aware of it.

Jesus spoke of our potential to influence others. He called us *salt* and *light*. We have been commissioned by God to use our time, resources, and abilities to impact the lives of others. God did not save us just to take us to heaven. I am grateful for the hope of heaven, but He also saved us to use us here on earth. That's why you have gifts, talents, and resources.

At times you will have no idea who you are influencing. Jennifer and I were at a wedding when a good friend of mine told me an encouraging story. He asked me if I remembered a fellow I went to college with in the late 80's or early 90's. I said I did, but I did not remember him very well. We were acquaintances who ran into each other occasionally. My friend proceeded to tell me that Brady, the guy he asked me about, had attempted to find me on a recent trip to South Georgia. I did not know it, but Brady had observed something about me while we attended college together. I literally had no idea he was watching. However, for some reason, He chose to name his son after me. I was floored to hear the news. I had not seen Brady in over a decade. That has always reminded me about the power of influence.

John Maxwell, years ago, defined leadership as *influence*. In other words, no matter your title, if you are not influencing others, you are not leading.

Few stories in the Bible give better illustration concerning the power of influence than David and Goliath. David's faith and courage moved others to get off the inactive list and get involved in the battle. Some who are on the sidelines of ministry may get on the playing field if you will lead.

The Bible says that once David fought Goliath, all those who were onlookers at the beginning of the story entered the battle. Suddenly, David was not in the battle alone. David's courage was not only instrumental in defeating the giant, but it also awakened the Israeli army out of its slumber. They got involved. Why? They were inspired by the actions of one. Again, *leadership is influence.* Look at how David influenced the soldiers.

> *Then David ran over and pulled Goliath's sword from its sheath. David used it to kill him and cut off his head. When the Philistines saw that their champion was dead, they turned and ran. Then the men of Israel and Judah gave a great shout of triumph and rushed after the Philistines, chasing them as far as Gath and the gates of Ekron. The bodies of the dead and wounded Philistines were strewn all along the road from Shaaraim, as far as Gath and Ekron.*
>
> — I Samuel 17:51-52 NLT

This shows how quickly things can change. The whole atmosphere was different. Those who had been filled with fear, all of the sudden, had courage. Those who fled now pursued. The hunted became the hunters. That is the difference one person, full of faith in God, can make.

David was like a spark. His faith and courage ignited determination in an army. A young, inexperienced shepherd boy displayed the kind of faith that reproduces itself, and so can you.

Full-grown men witnessed a young boy with faith do what no one else had even dared to try. David, armed with a sling and rocks, had revealed the fear that filled them but also inspired them to action. David, the shepherd of those few sheep. David, the one too young to win the battle. David, the one forgotten the day Samuel came to anoint the 2nd King of Israel. God used the improbable to do the impossible.

David gave hope to the hopeless. His presence refreshed the downcast army. None of them got involved as long as David was talking about what he was going to do. It was action that stirred the soldiers. Stated intentions do not always bring a following, but courageous action is contagious. You can influence others to action as well.

It was that moment that the man who had so effectively led sheep became a leader of people. He earned respect by acting on his convictions. His courage touched hearts. What they saw in him gave them hope for themselves and Israel.

The Israeli army was *dead in the valley* until David, the least likely candidate, arrived. The soldiers did not need more weapons and the army did not need more soldiers. They did not need more training. They needed a leader! They did not need a man with a title of General. Titles don't overcome discouragement. Titles don't win battles that never should be won. Titles don't inspire. Leaders do all three.

Influence means making a noticeable difference in someone else's life. To influence someone is to bring some sort of change to them. As Christians, this is what our lives should be doing. With love and faith filling our hearts, we should be influencing others for the cause of Christ.

Parents have great influence on children. Teachers greatly impact students. Coaches have lifetime impact in the lives of athletes. Regardless of position, you can have a positive, Godly influence on those around you.

I will never forget the impact one of my college professors had on my life. Mrs. Mixon was a lady who dripped with southern grace and charm. She was the perfect teacher for the most imperfect students. As I have already stated, for several years I was not a model student. However, the words and love of Mrs. Mixon influenced me greatly.

Mrs. Mixon became a part of my life as a result of academic expulsion from Abraham Baldwin Agricultural College. I went there to play baseball. I guess I assumed they would let me play without going to class. After flunking out due to a cumulative GPA of 0.7, I was mandated by a probation board to take a class that was designed to make me a better student.

Standing at the door the first day of class was Mrs. Mixon. She was elegant looking and had a certain presence about her that made me feel more comfortable than I would have otherwise. She had her work cut out for her, but she was cut out for the work. Her assignment was to teach/inspire an entire class of students on probation to greater things. I venture to say that not only did none of us have academic goals, we did not have goals of any kind. Besides that, most of us had already done so much damage to our GPA's, we had little chance anyway. This was no ordinary class. She was no ordinary teacher. Thank God!

Being in the class was part of my probation. In essence, that meant I had one more chance. So, I, along with many other students assigned to the course by an appeals board, filed into Mrs. Mixon's class. As we entered the room, Mrs. Mixon handed each one of us a replica of a bumble bee. I had no idea, all these years later, that I would still remember such an experience. But, as odd as it sounds, that little bumblebee impacted my life.

Mrs. Mixon started the class by asking us to put the bumblebee on our desks. Then, in her gracious southern accent she said, *Every time you see this bumblebee, I want you to remember, you can 'bee' all you want to 'bee.'* If reading that makes you feel embarrassed, how do you think a room full of fresh flunkies were feeling upon hearing that? I was humiliated. I didn't even want to look at anyone else. But while I wanted to disappear into thin air, I could not escape the sincerity of Mrs. Mixon. She believed it. In hindsight, I can see that she was giving each of us something we needed: hope. She did not see us as problem students. Rather, she looked at us as opportunities for her to make a difference. And she did.

Leadership can be tough business. There is tremendous reward in influencing others, but there is also sacrifice. To be a leader who makes a positive difference in this world, like David, you must *lose yourself* for a greater cause. This simply means you must live for more than yourself. There was a period of time David had little, if any, support. Others eventually came alongside him, but that certainly was not the case in the beginning.

Are you using all God has given you to influence others? Jesus did. Of course, He was, and will always be, the greatest leader who ever lived. Consider Peter, a rugged fisherman. Jesus influenced Peter in such a way that took him from his lifelong job as a fisherman to becoming the preacher used to preach the sermon on The Day of Pentecost. That sermon launched the Church into existence. No doubt, we would consider Paul to be an influential person in church history. By divine inspiration, much of the New Testament is under his authorship. His influence had not always been for good, though. At one time, Paul, then Saul, hated

Christians. With his prestigious background as a student of Gamalial and his reputation as a Pharisee of Pharisees, he generated major disruption for Christ followers until an experience untangled him from the cords of legalism.

Acts 9 teaches what happened when Paul came under the influence of grace. The pride and hatred in his heart met its match as he neared Demascus and uniquely encountered Jesus Christ. The man determined to destroy Christianity was turned into a soldier of the love and grace of God.

Jesus knew we would live in a dark world, so He commanded us to be light. He even refers to us as *the light of the world* (Matthew 5:14). The long, dark shadow of depravity on this planet is evident. Sickness and sorrow, disease and death, and all sorts of injustice permeate this world of darkness. But, that's why there is a need for light. With that understanding, Jesus commissioned all who call themselves *Christians* to use their influence for Him. God has even given us His Spirit to enable us to bear fruit to display His character. His Spirit provides power so that His supernatural works can happen in and through our lives. He desires for the difference He has made in our lives to be used to make a difference in the lives of others. It's called influence.

I believe the greatest New Testament example of this is the story of Jesus and the demoniac (Luke 8:26-29). If you have ever wanted to see what the devil does to a life he controls, just read the story. This man lived in a graveyard, naked and tormented. Demonically possessed, he could not even be held by shackles and chains. After a short encounter with Jesus, the demons were cast into a herd of pigs and the man was,

> *Clothed and in his right mind.*
>
> — Luke 8:35 NASB

But I want you to see what happened after his deliverance. The Bible says,

> *The man who had been freed from the demons begged to go with Him.*
>
> — Luke 26:38 NLT

That's understandable. Who would not make the same request? But Jesus' answer is startling:

'No, go back to your family, and tell them everything God has done for you.' So, he went through the town proclaiming the great things Jesus had done for him.

— Luke 8:39 NLT

Request denied! Jesus wanted the man to use his story to influence his family and the communities who had seen him suffer all those years. In other words, his greatest influence would not be on the other side of the Sea of Galilee. He could make the biggest impact where people could see the difference God had made in his life. It's the difference that makes the difference.

As Christians, we influence with words and actions. Just as David spoke his convictions and acted on them, so must we. Those who give God lip service, but have little action to substantiate their words, do not serve as light. The Bible says in I John 3:18,

Dear children, let's not merely say that we love each other; let us show the truth by our actions.

NLT

You can make a difference. Your attitude can influence those who work around you. No matter your age or gender, a healthy dose of humility and boldness can produce light that will greatly impact others for their good and God's glory. Our good works do not save us, but they are instrumental in others being saved for the glory of God:

> *In the same way, let your good deeds shine out for all to see, so that everyone will praise your Heavenly Father.*
>
> — Matthew 5:16 NLT

Chapter 8

The Heart of the Matter

Having preached from the story of David and Goliath many times, I wanted the answer to these questions, *What was the key to David's victory? Why did he rise to the top even though he was the youngest and least qualified? Why was it that a young boy, running a mundane errand for his father, ended up being victorious against all odds? Was it that he had divine awareness, or was it his ability to overcome discouragement and criticism?* The answer was none of these alone. Rather, it was the heart of the man.

Let's end where we started by looking at the importance of the heart. I sincerely believe the reason for David's victory is found all the way back in Chapter 16 of I Samuel. This is where we see the spiritual X-ray from God on David. God saw what no one else could see.

I once heard Dr. Mark Rutland say, *the heart of the matter is the matter of the heart.* How true! The Scripture bears out that God was extremely pleased with the heart of David. The book of Acts states,

> *But God removed Saul and replaced him with David, a man about whom God said, 'I have found David son of Jesse, a man after my own heart. He will do everything I want him to do.'*

> — Acts 13:22 NLT

It was David's heart — not his skill, ability, or background — that opened the door for him to enter as king of Israel.We looked at this verse in the opening chapter, but it is worth another look:

But the Lord said to Samuel,

> *'Don't judge by his appearance or height, for I have rejected him. The Lord does not see things the way you see them. People judge by outward appearance, but the Lord looks at the heart.'*

> — I Samuel 16:7 NLT

David's heart was not a deciding factor for God; it was the deciding factor in God anointing him as king. God proves to us that He is unimpressed with what often impresses us.

Hard-hearted people are difficult to deal with. And nothing hardens the heart like pride. The field of history is littered with individuals who have hardened their hearts toward God and suffered the consequences. A hard heart resists God and His love.

The term *hard-hearted* creates a clear word picture. God's love cannot grow in hard hearts, because the seed of His Word cannot find fertile ground. This is why many hear the Word without receiving it. Hard hearts are resistant and shed everything Godly, like water pounding against a steel wall.

Imagine trying to plant a garden on a slab of concrete. The sound of plows scraping off the concrete reflects the experience of many people when faced with the Word and Spirit of God. Throwing a seed on a slab of concrete is a waste of time. In the same way, the Word of God must land in culti-vated hearts to produce fruit. Jesus illus-trates this in the parable of the soils. Mark 4:5-6 says,

'Other seed fell on shallow soil
with underlying rock. The seed
sprouted quickly because the soil
was shallow. But the plant soon
wilted under the hot sun, and
since it didn't have deep roots,
it died.'

NLT

I suppose there are numerous reasons people become hard-hearted. Some of the most hard-hearted people are found in church or have been raised in church. It shows you can develop a habit for attending church without developing a heart for God. The most hard-hearted people in the Bible spent much of their time in the temple and synagogues. They were known as Pharisees, and their hard hearts were seldom penetrated. Year after year their hearts were petrified with spiritual pride. Legalists have little, if any, desire to see a lost and hurting world come to faith in Christ. They would rather be sure the by-laws of the church are being strictly observed and church traditions are being sustained. Those with hard hearts often add years of church attendance without spiritually maturing. They prove it is possible to grow old without growing up. Growth is not possible for these people.

The seed of God's Word cannot find fertile ground to flourish in.

There are those who have been offended by the church and have become hard hearted. Due to pastoring for many years, I have seen people leave churches with hearts of stone. Some carry their baggage to other churches, while others become part of the crowd famous for saying, *I don't have to go to church to be a Christian.* Technically, they're right. But too often, they're only justifying disobedience. It is not uncommon to hear someone speak of an individual who once served God faithfully in the local church but got angry at the preacher or someone who did not meet his/her expectations. I implore you, *guard your heart!*

If I were to ask you, *How would you like for your life to be filled with joy, peace, patience, kindness, gentleness, and things like these?* Well, if you would like to have a life filled with these characteristics, IT IS POSSIBLE! But these spiritual blessings are not for the hard-hearted. Consider what Jesus teaches about how important the Word of God is when it comes to living a fruitful life.

'The seed that fell on good soil represents those who truly hear and understand God's Word and produce a harvest of thirty, sixty, or even a hundred times as much as had been planted.'

— Matthew 13:23 NLT

Fertile, cultivated hearts are the landscape for healthy, productive lives.

The heart is Grand Central Station. Ponder on this verse,

As a face is reflected in water, so the heart reflects the real person.

— Proverbs 27:19 NLT

When God speaks of the heart, He is speaking of the essence of who we truly are. It is where God detects phoniness, hypocrisy, and vain religion. It is also where He detects humility, gratefulness, and faith.

The physical heart has obvious importance. Blood is essential for life, and it takes the heart to get blood to all the right places. You will never have a checkup with your physician where he/she does not place his/her stethoscope over your heart. One of the most moving experiences for a parent is hearing the heartbeat of a child while in its mother's womb.

There is no question that God checks our hearts. This Old Testament verse says it all,

> *The eyes of the Lord search the whole earth in order to strengthen those whose hearts are fully committed to Him.*

> — II Chronicles 16:9 NLT

Paul teaches that it is God's work in the heart that pleases Him.

> *No, a true Jew is one whose heart is right with God. And true circumcision is not merely obeying the letter of the law; rather, it is a change of heart produced by the Spirit. And a person with a changed heart seeks praise from God, not from people.*

> — Romans 2:29 NLT

God specializes in seeing to it that those who stand proudly on their pedestals of pride come down. Yet, those who humble themselves are greatly blessed of the Lord and exalted. Consider these verses,

> *But those who exalt themselves will be humbled, and those who humble themselves will be exalted.*
>
> — Matthew 23:12 NLT

> *True humility and fear of the Lord lead to riches, honor, and long life.*
>
> — Proverbs 22:4 NLT

Peter wrote,

> *In the same way, you who are younger must accept the authority of the elders. And all of you, dress yourselves in humility as you relate to one another, for 'God opposes the proud but gives grace to the humble.' So humble yourselves under the mighty power of God, and at the right time He will lift you up in honor.*
>
> — I Peter 5:5-6 NLT

Lack of humility before God is a heart problem. I once heard a preacher say, *Some preachers are so prideful they can strut sitting down.* Hear this! You can either step off the shaky pedestal of pride onto a solid foundation, or someday, some way, you will get knocked off. Your arrogance that laughs in the face of God will cease and be replaced with bitter tears. In fact, ultimately, everyone will be humbled before the Lord. Philippians 2:9-11 says,

> *So that at the name of Jesus every knee will bow, of those who are in heaven and on earth and under the earth, and that every tongue will confess that Jesus Christ is Lord, to the glory of God the Father.*

> NASB

Why not humble yourself today? Jesus taught that we should love God with our whole heart. James taught us to humble our hearts before God. David was chosen because of his heart. As Hannah prayed for a son, the Bible records her words as,

> *'I haven't been drinking wine or anything stronger. But I am very*

discouraged, and I was pouring out my heart to the Lord.'

> — I Samuel 1:15 NLT

As Mary the mother of Jesus watched the shepherds come into the manger to see her newborn son, the Bible says,

But Mary kept all these things in her heart and thought about them often.

> — Luke 2:19 NLT

Jesus also said,

God blesses those whose hearts are pure, for they will see God.

> — Matthew 5:8 NLT

Those who have a heart for God love Him. Having a pure heart that is cultivated and not hard is essential for use on the battlefield of the Christian life. David stuck out that day. Eliab, Saul, and Goliath all made the same mistake: they placed far too much confidence in what they could see. They could see that Goliath was old and David was young. They could see Goliath was big and David was small. They could see Goliath had the armor of a seasoned warrior and David had a shepherd's bag and little more. However, they failed to consider the power of what they could not see: David's heart.

David had the heart of a champion. Some of you remember the song, *Eye of the Tiger*. It was a song of motivation, victory, and overcoming. What about David, though? Did he have the *Eye of the Tiger*? Was his eye the key to victory? No, it was not his eye but his heart.

I guess I am exhausting the issue of the heart because almost a decade ago (as I write this) this concept saved our marriage. At the brink of divorce, my wife and I were blessed to fall under the teaching of those who understood that the best way to change a home is to change the hearts that occupy it. Since then, we have attempted to share this amazing principle with as many people as possible: *the course of your life is determined by the condition of your heart*.

> *Guard your heart above all else, for it determines the course of your life.*
>
> Proverbs 4:23 NLT

111

As I close, I want to remind us all that there is a key to David's victory. It was not that he had the heart of a lion. So, what was his heart like?

It is in that question we find the true reason for David's victory over Goliath. His was not the heart of a lion. His was the heart of a child.

This is where we often miss it. The child-like faith and humility we possess at the point of salvation can give way to a faith that has less to do with heartfelt service and more to do with a sense of duty. Jesus taught that those who worship God must worship Him in *spirit and in truth* (John 4:24). We have to guard against allowing the softness of our hearts at the time of salvation slowly hardening due to the devices and deceit of Satan and the allures of this world.

When I was much younger, I would travel to my hometown to see my nephew, Buck. It was only a seventeen-mile drive. When he was born, we all thought the earth ceased its rotation around the sun and started rotating around him. We would laugh and play together. His innocence and love touched me in an unusual way. There was a couch that sat in front of a large window of their house. I will never forget leaving from seeing him one particular day. As I backed out, I looked back at the house to that window that faced the driveway. Buck, so small, had worked his way onto the couch to wave goodbye. I was overwhelmed with his childlike love. It was in my vehicle immediately following that incident that I sensed God's Spirit speak to my heart and reveal to me that He desires to be loved with a childlike heart. Buck taught me so much all those years ago. I wish I could say I have lived with a childlike heart every day since. I can't. But I can still remember it like it was yesterday. Since that experience with Buck, Jennifer and I have had the blessing of seeing three little girls (Alora Gail, KenLee, and Dempsey Anna) come into the world. As small children, there were moments they helped me understand Matthew 18:2-4,

Jesus called a little child to Him and put the child among them. Then He said, 'I tell you the truth, unless you turn from your sins and become like little children, you will never get into the kingdom of Heaven. So, anyone who becomes as humble as this little

*child is greatest in the Kingdom
of Heaven.'*

NLT

Strip your pride, peel off your arrogance, and come before God with childlike faith. He has plans for you. On the day David stepped onto the battlefield, the warrior was a child. David knew in his heart that God was for him and with him. His heart was clean. His motives were right. He was usable. He was focused on God, not Goliath. From David's perspective, Goliath was standing in the long shadow of God.

Be sure of this: all the taunting and intimidating voices you have ever heard can be cast under the same shadow if you will humble your heart, and, by faith, give your *Goliaths* to God.

CPSIA information can be obtained
at www.ICGtesting.com
Printed in the USA
BVHW081751090919

557952BV00014B/1931/P